CW01647484

Persephone in Finsbury Park

Persephone in Finsbury Park

Myra Schneider

Second Light Publications

Persephone in Finsbury Park

First published 2016 by
Second Light Publications
3 Springfield Close
East Preston
West Sussex
BN16 2SZ

info@secondlightlive.co.uk
www.secondlightlive.co.uk

ISBN 978-0-9927088-2-5

Printed and bound by TJ International Limited, Padstow, Cornwall, PL28 8RW
Cover artwork by Martin Parker
Designed by Martin Parker at www.silbercow.co.uk

Typeset in Minion 12.75pt & 11.5pt

PREVIOUS TITLES

Poetry

Fistful of Yellow Hope, Littlewood Press 1984
Cat Therapy, Littlewood Press 1986
Cathedral of Birds, Littlewood/Giant Steps 1988
Opening The Ice, (with Ann Dancy) Smith/Doorstop 1990
Crossing Point, Littlewood Press1991
Exits, Enitharmon 1991
The Panic Bird, Enitharmon 1998
Insisting on Yellow: New and Selected Poems, Enitharmon 2000
Multiplying The Moon, Enitharmon 2004
Becoming, Second Light Publications 2007
Circling The Core, Enitharmon 2008
What Women Want, Second Light Publications 2012
The Door to Colour, Enitharmon 2014

Prose

Marigold's Monster, Heinemann 1976
If Only I Could Walk, Heinemann 1977
Will The Real Pete Roberts Stand Up, Heinemann 1978
Writing for Self-Discovery with John Killick, Element Books 1998
Writing for Self-Discovery, republished Vega 2002
Writing My Way Through Cancer, Jessica Kingsley 2003
Writing Your Self with John Killick, Continuum International 2009

As Co-Editor

Parents, Enitharmon 2000
Making Worlds, Headland 2003
Four Caves Of The Heart, Second Light Publications 2004
Images of Women, Arrowhead Press 2006
Her Wings of Glass, Second Light Publications 2014

ACKNOWLEDGEMENTS

Poems in this collection have previously appeared in:

Acumen, ARTEMISpoetry, POEM magazine, Frogmore Papers, Quadrant, Scintilla.

The First of Spring and *His Gift from Brazil* are in *At Time's Edge*, 2016, a special memorial volume of *Scintilla* to commemorate poet, Anne Cluysenaar

Margaret is reprinted from *Circling The Core*, Enitharmon Press 2008

I would like to thank Dilys Wood for her support of my work and for her in-depth feedback on *Persephone in Finsbury Park* and other long poems. I also want to thank John Killick who has given me feedback on most of my poems since 1982, Caroline Price for detailed comments on the poems I find most tricky, Mimi Khalvati for her belief in my work and insightful feedback, the Sunday workshop group and also Justina Hart, Alyss Dye and Hannah Salter who all read *Persephone in Finsbury Park* and offered useful suggestions. A special thank you to Martin Parker for his splendid cover design and production work.

Importantly, I want to thank Erwin Schneider, my husband for his practical help and giving me space to write over many years and also my main publisher, Stephen Stuart-Smith as well as Isabel Brittain and their small band of dedicated workers for their encouragement and support. I also want to thank Les Murray who has published poems of mine in *Quadrant* over a long period of time.

CONTENTS

THE FIRST OF SPRING

for Anne Cluysenaar

A honey sun, the cease of gnawing wind
so we seize the day, unleash ourselves
in the country park, gaze at flowers inscribed *To Dad*

lying on a bench. They summon a huge bee
to their pink and yellow freesia bells. Dreamily,
I too enter the nectar-laden chambers and feed.

Turning away, we follow *the droghte of March* track
to the water garden where snowdrops are fading,
daffodils are on the brink of opening

and expectation's in bloom on naked trees.
Welters of lily stalks in the darks of a pond
are tangles of umbilical cords. Beyond the garden,

beyond the singing of birds is a lake which glitters
as if it's a source of light. We sit down
on a wicker seat and there you are breathing

in the budding warmth, freed from the last
of October now and that distressed message
you sent before your life was snatched.

You're stooping over a small plant, stroking
its leaves, tracking the hover-rise of a damselfly,
smiling as you follow all the riverlets.

WINGS

The wings you spy hovering above the sweep
of naked sand are black flappers
with turkey-gobble heads. Ruthless
as the sun, you know they'll swoop,
scrawny necks outstretched, wrap themselves
round your body, squeeze
your breath and their beaks will pierce
your flesh to the heart.

The wings you glimpse in the dusk-laden copse
fold away as their owner alights
on a branch above your head.
The creature embodies such stillness
not a leaf stirs and the moons it stole
from the sky to plant in its hollowed face,
stare through your soul, pull you unresisting,
into its unearthly world.

The dusky wings you see flocking hollyhocks
and bee-milked lavenders in a garden
shelving down to a river dreaming away
the afternoon, belong to fluttering peacocks
whose eyespots are hypnotic circles
of sapphire, violet, lemon. One nestles
on your foot probing for nectar and you take on
its lightness of being.

HOW TO FIND WEIGHTLESSNESS

for John

Not watching a black and white film extolling
the way of life of a sect who embrace mobiles
and other technologies but whose daily lives
are shaped by centuries-old ritual and rules
which relegate women to marriage and child-rearing.
You long for the heroine to defy a decree constricting
as binding the feet of Chinese girls once was.

Not emerging into a drizzling December night
only to be mocked by a lit shop window displaying
a cornucopia of gaudy porcelain fruit, glass pigs
in polka dot skirts and a bag labelled 'elephant nude'
which slaps before you again that photo of a market
in Burma crammed with stalls selling animal parts –
one heaped with pieces hacked from elephant hide.

Not hovering outside the tube station where everyone
is ignoring the man crouched by its garnet-red tiles.
No sign he's begging but his youthful face is worn
as an old retriever's, his teeth are chattering.
Not following your partner through the ticket barrier,
ashamed that you too have passed by, not suffering
the squeezebox of unknown bodies in the train.

But at last, closing the door on the smack of wind
and wet, you lie down on a carpet upstairs, stretch
each leg upwards in turn. As they lighten, loosen,
the burden of body and thought falls away
and above you the sphere shading the electric bulb
turns into the sun's golden orb. Weightless,
you float easily as a balloon towards blue warmth.

/...

Of course if you escaped gravity you'd be pitched
into the dark of the immense void beyond Earth
and shrivel but who can face reality, its granite layers,
without finding some space to drift into illusion?
Forgetting physics you soar above the South Downs –
those slopes and scarps you roamed as a girl,
listen to the exultation flowing from a dot of lark.

3 AM

I'm moonless as tonight's sky, helpless
as a rabbit's blind and furless kits
and in my body's cave misgivings hang
from the walls like folded wings. To combat

thumping pain and racing fear, I picture
a Matisse-red room with French windows,
potted palms and a half-naked woman
lounging on a sofa, then the yellow surprise

of the first drifts of daffodils trumpeting
spring to morose February this morning.
It doesn't work and the silence is implacable
as the dark – I wish it purred like the cat settling

her warm self into the curve of my spine
to sleep but the black cat has long gone.
A tremble in the air – and there are my friends,
shadowy at first beyond my bed. Their outlines

slowly fill out with muted colours and now
they're facing each other in two rows
as if for a formal dance. They reach out,
join hands across the divide. I gaze

at their arms which seem to form the ribs
of a boat, the kind ancient kings were buried in
but this is no death ship – it's a hammock
they've made for me. The moment I lie down

it takes my body's burden. No one speaks
but touch has its own language. I let go
of distress and feel such lightness of being
I could lift off into the blue like a damselfly.

PURE

The silk spun from a worm,
the sea's forget-me-not blue, a newly
born human unmarked by the world,
the word queening a hoarding
and slyly inserted in the caption underneath:
A Life of Pure Style and Indulgence.
                                                            To whet
the appetite a photo of a room juts into sky.
I note the polished floor, slender-legged lamps,
faux leather furniture, insistent wall screen,
picture window – no welcoming pet,
pot plant, teapot, open book.
                                        What's pure,
I ask the paving stones, about stirring up desire
to wine and dine expensively while watching
pulp TV in a room concocted in an office
by a designer who knows exactly
how to tempt today's buyers?
                                                        What's pure,
I ask a litter bin, about a set of apartments
opposite a car park that's next to a station fronted
by a pull-in for buses, a set of apartments
which rubs shoulders with the rail track and faces
a street where vehicles queue to join
a manic motorway?
                                            What's pure
I ask a lamp post about twisting the meaning
out of yet another word? Think: *nice, pretty,*
awesome, devastating, precisely, each lifeless
as a mouse the cat's finished with.
                                                            Pure! the word
tolls as I leave the judder in the main road
and trot down to the park, rest my eyes
on trees offering the froth of blossom,
stare at the clot of log, plastic wrappers,
wire coils, chucked cans and lumps of paper
which are jamming the Brook.

ALDEBURGH IN AUGUST

Faint wings of sails are perched on the sea
where it pools into sky, all that blue
which insists it won't end – you don't want it to.
Such a frisking of light on the shingle beach,
such a letting go in marigold and peach,
in laughter and screech as waves pounce on toes.
Gulls on the make are stationed on hulls and bonnets
of snoozing cars. Up on the esplanade,
black as crows, fishermen's shacks – they've sold out
of crab and skate. Adults bask like seals
on benches, a raspberry-capped van is doing
hot business in cooling kids. Today
even pansies in formal beds are wallowing
in heat. You try to pretend wrangling, bombing,
destitution are thousands of miles away.

DECEMBER

The day's so lightless you wonder why it bothered
to crawl from bed and worse, winter's stripped
the trees of leaves. They stand on the icy ground,
their naked arms raised as if begging
to be clothed in warmth. It's now that damp
reveals itself beneath kitchen sinks and mould
flourishes on the walls of draughty rooms in old
ill-treated houses. You try to hoard
the colour of heaped oranges, scarlet berries,
silver paper, the gold of finches flickering
among branches but you can't forget –
even when you see the woodpecker alight
with moss-green wings and cap red as hope –
that need is wealth's neighbour and struggling to cope.

THE SWEDE

More like a deformed animal than part of a plant,
I imagine it snuffling in the dark, dreaming itself
a globe as it heaves against waterlogged clay and stones

to fill out its girth. Hard as mahogany, heavy as flint,
its thick skin is marked with blotches purple as bruise,
ringed with ridges. This one has an outgrowth

that's like a foetal limb. At first I brand the vegetable
inferior to the leeks I dug up in the garden one year,
each smooth as a pole and more whitely alive than snow

but the ungainly body speaks of persistent labour,
quiet confidence, gravitas, and I admire it for making
no pretence to be other than it is. I begin to wonder why

we're so careless of the earth which coddles seedlings,
coaxes them to reach for the light and harbours
their weighty fruit, why we're forever looking up at the sky,

probing Mars for signs of life, seeking out ever fainter galaxies
and, as the mystery of space-time grows, why we keep
trying to crack the secret which began the universe.

Better to consider the casserole we're having for supper,
how when I lift the glass-lidded pot out of the oven
slow cooking will have turned the pieces of swede

luminous orange and soft enough to slip down
the throat, warm the belly. Better to ask how long
it will be before the swede's an endangered species.

HIS GIFT FROM BRAZIL

for Ben

is enclosed in a wooden box that's weighty and inviting
as Pandora's. I can't wait to prise open its neatly planed lid.

Inside, dark as the deepest amber masking the death-sprawl
of the insect it trapped millennia ago when it was a pool of resin,

is a superior preserve which would frown at jam trickling
down the side of its container. Like the opinionated, it refuses

to budge but I manage to dig out a spoonful and spread it thickly
over melting butter on the pocked surface of a crumpet.

The first bite is into the softest cushion of utter sweetness.
It tastes of petals flaring on flame trees, paradise flowers,

parrot plumage, the green ferment of foliage and frond,
of shade pulsing with insects and weird spirits yet it's mellow

as English sunlight in late September, as the first yellowing
of long-fingered leaves on the sycamores beyond my garden.

The second bite tastes of unstoppable abundance, sends me
out to the sunflowers, giants who sprang up in summer, ghosts now.

Their huge heads gripped by green claws dwarf my hand's span.
They're brittle – a piece breaks off from one. It's bristly as a broom

but it houses so many nutritious seeds in its cells I could harvest
these ghosts, plant the needy world with chrome and ochre glory.

/…

The last bite tastes of healing. I dream this delicacy is quietening
my mind, easing stubborn joints, enriching blood as it flows

round my body, feeding overdry skin like rain moistening
starved ground. Suddenly I see those hallelujahs of luminous gold

which stream from sun and horizon in a late Turner watercolour
where sea and sky are inseparable. Gently, I close the wooden box.

BREATHING SPACE

It might begin anytime, anywhere:
on Hungerford Bridge say where, slung
above the Thames, you could flap arms
in the blue if the wind wasn't frisking your body.
But maybe it starts in the darkening street
so thronged with cold even noise
is freezing up as you pick out
a punnet of plump cherries
and the mittened stallholder says:
Here you are darling, keep warm,
for you find you're letting go of breath
you'd no idea you'd been holding.

Joining the tide of tired bodies,
you descend the too-long escalator,
squeeze into a carriage, thank
your lucky stars for a seat, close
your eyes, see the shine of those *keep-warm*,
ebony cherries, inhabit their roundness,
their ripeness, breathe in slow, slow.
Your throat unbuttons, the corset of ribs
loosens, air travels all your passageways
and for once you don't hurry it out,
for once you encounter those lost-bird circlings
instead of driving them into the mind's corners.
As soon as they have space they quieten.

/...

Ready now for the world's multiplicities,
you try to read the face of the woman
opposite. Not young, she has a glint
in her eyes that's almost amusement
and signals she's still in the swim.
You can't take your eyes off her purple shoes
criss-crossed with pink laces or the rise
of substantial legs, twins in black tights –
legs which certain early creatures
acquired millennia ago and used to crawl
out of the sea, legs which suddenly
seem amazing when you consider
that ammonites are your distant ancestors.

You're gazing at other samples of legs
humans have evolved and nibbling
a cherry when the train jerks to a stop
at your station. You slip the breathing space
into your bag, step onto the platform.

SUNDAY MORNING IN THE PARK

I'm weaving between willows trailing the stream,
joggers, wobblers on bikes, snouts engrossed
in sniffing when a voice calls: *Lily!* At once I dream

cream and magenta lily blooms belling
the sultry air and spotted tiger lilies,
their long-stamened mouths slowly opening

to kiss passing sleeves and insects with saffron.
Lily, here! A mild request rather than an order.
Before me appears a Pre-Raphaelite maiden

with a pallid face and cascading gold hair,
then, robed in white, the slender Lady of Shallot
in a boat that's ferrying her down an innocent river.

Lily! The feeble attempt to be assertive recalls me
to twists of broken boughs, nettles and the fact
that the character being addressed has a roly-poly,

unlovely body slung low above the ground,
a face tapering to a wolfish muzzle, a muddy
brown coat. I gape – so utterly 'unlily', this hound

which clearly intends to continue gorging on smells
by the dirty water. Its stooping elderly owner
puts a leaflet in my hand. *Do come*, she smiles.

I nod, skirt a tricycle and an overweight man
in shorts straining to do keep fit, glance
at the paper: *Canine Capers: a Day of Fun.*

Lily! Patience is beginning to evaporate now.
I try to picture Lily's behaviour on the festive day –
an animal less likely to caper than a pig is to fly!

ANNE ASKEW

For refusing to be muzzled by her husband
as other wives were and striking out on her own path,
for her quick educated mind, her ability to discourse with learned men,
I shall remember her.

For her resolve to go to London, seek out thinkers
and interpret the bible, risky even though the king by taking
the title Supreme Head of the Church, had opened the door to enquiry,
I shall remember her.

For her passionate preaching of the gospels,
for not being cowed when arrested and thrown into prison
but refuting the persecutors who tried to force-feed her Catholic beliefs,
I shall remember her.

For her canny evasions and logical arguments,
for answering tartly when the stricture was hurled: 'A woman
has no more business with the scriptures than a sow has wearing a saddle',
I shall remember her.

For expounding metaphors in the Bible:
'We are not to take Christ as the material thing by which
he's signified for then we would make him a door, a lamb, a vine, a stone…',
I shall remember her.

For the fire, not the fire built up at Smithfield
but that fire in her belly that gave her strength to endure
the rack which wrenched her shoulders and hips out of their sockets,
I shall remember her.

For the fire which inspired her poems
and writings about her trials, the fire which made her hold fast
as the awed crowd gasped and unstoppable flames snatched at her flesh,
I shall remember her.

Anne Askew: 1521–1546. The 1534 Act of Supremacy granted Henry VIII Royal Supremacy which meant he was declared The Supreme Head of the Church in England.

THE REAL MRS BEETON

Heaving her enormous bulk onto a bookshelf high
above my bed, then pushing until she was out of sight
took all my strength and it didn't dislodge her from my mind.

But I rebelled against the weight of her disapproval,
shut myself away every morning in that small room
of my own, the room which is me, to let imagination

run wild as brambles and grasses in an untended garden,
coaxed visions into scribblings on paper until desk
and floor were littered until, unblinking as owl eyes,

words stared from my screen. Of course, the moment
I emerged I came face to face with her large a life
on the landing. For years this matron, large-bosomed

and with a voluminous knowledge gathered from decades
of managing a household, followed me around tutting
because I hadn't blanched or basted, couldn't pluck a duck.

She snorted at unruly children sliding down the stairs,
at dust rollicking along skirting boards, rounded on me
for failing to keep a properly stocked linen cupboard.

Then the day I found out this paragon was Isabella Beeton,
a young woman who, instead of devoting her life to home
and family like other Victorian wives, travelled by train

with her publisher husband to his London office, wrote
books fat with information, mostly magpied from other books,
about household management, became a money-spinner,

an authority for later generations. I also learnt she'd suffered
several miscarriages, bore two children who died in infancy,
two who survived, died herself after the second –

thanks to Mr Beeton's syphilis. Yet for years books
in her name continued to appear. The matron's ghost
still persists in my mind but what troubles me is Isabella.

For all the thousands of pages this woman produced
in her short life, the *real Mrs Beeton* didn't leave
a single word about what she thought, felt, endured.

REBECCA

Somewhere inside me: snippets from her life,
that village a dozen miles from Vitebsk, the cows
she knew by heart, the grocery shop and pogroms

left behind for a cramped existence in Stepney:
families living elbow to elbow, her six-year old Judith
scalded to death tipping water from a boiling kettle.

These scraps and others are in a bundle much smaller
than the bundle of linens she heaved through years
of unpaved streets after her husband died,

selling on the never-never. There's little Isaac
who couldn't keep still for a moment, never allowed
indoors on his own – such harm might he come to –

playing outside till her day's slog was over, in winter
at the mercy of frost which sank its teeth so deep
into his legs the bite was still raw ninety years later.

There's the tale of how she dug her needle wit
into the boy for fooling in his new secondary school,
being placed twenty-ninth, then of how proud she was

when he became, not the rabbi she'd dreamed of
in the tiny bedroom they shared for years,
but such a scholar he was paid to go to university.

Rebecca, grandmother I never knew, your son
always called you *mother* – I didn't learn your name
until seven years after he died – I'm proud of *you*.

MARGARET

Larder's a misnomer for this kitchen cupboard
with wooden shelves hidden by creased fablon, with vents
that admit air from our London garden and far beyond.

Our so-called larder stores no coolth – how could it,
wedded to a wall facing south onto a terrace that mimics
Africa when summer bursts out? Real larders, like the one

in your house, Margaret, have marble shelves, walls thick
as the length of an arm, a shaded window. It takes seconds
to step back decades and lift the muslin cover

from the wide-lipped jug. Your house echoed the larder:
passages with overflowing bookcases, a roomy kitchen,
the comforting quiet of lounge sofas – a quiet that grew

from you. Ginger-haired, wide-hipped and flat-faced,
you weren't outwardly beautiful but pale girls
who were shut up in borstals would run to hug you

whenever you visited. You were beautiful to them,
to me too when my teens ended and, lost in the world,
I failed my parents' expectations. Dear Margaret,

you cupboarded such kindness, offered me
a refuge from judgement. And yet you told me in old age
you had always felt yourself to be a misfit in the world.

MRS PRICE

Mrs. Price did for us in the 1880s house where we lived
at the beginning of our marriage. She looked as if
she'd been born worn out and in a headscarf,

always arrived with her eyes popping out, needed
to *sit dear for a minute and have a cup of tea.*
Once she'd got her breath back she spilt the latest news:

blood pouring when a car ran over *her at number ten*,
the police at the door pestering with nasty questions,
him at number three doing the dirty on his wife and kids.

Worser and worser, she'd blurt, her bird head jerking
from side to side. The Daily Mirror, its shocking stories,
were a staple too though its pages ended their short lives

spread out on the floors she washed, to help them dry.
Not on the phone, so if she was feeling bad she was simply
missing from our Monday kitchen and it had a dull morning.

Once, after a gap I went to St. Ann's Road. She grabbed me
by the arm, face whiter than usual and packed with fear,
led me to her front room. It was spick, dimly brown, threadbare.

They're knocking down our street, putting us all away
in them dreadful flats. Pointless to list stainless steel kitchen,
cream white rooms, a bathroom with taps shining like stars.

The neighbours, in calling distance and always ready
to chew disasters over and over, were her daily bread.
But what did the mighty *they* care about tearing lives apart?

THE WORD

I awaken muddled, to slovenly bedclothes,
the blur-grey of drizzle. Back and legs are sluggish.
Difficult to pretend I'm not getting old –
yesterday's visitor rubbed it in as she smiled

at our wallpaper: *lovely sixties – pity it's out of date.*
Unbirthday weather but I set out with self
and presents swaddled in layers of plastic.
Serious rain at Finsbury Park so I stick

my head into the dim of the minicab office
instead of trudging to the flock of dozing buses.
The spectacled woman behind the desk is dipping
bread into a carton of winter vegetable soup

in spite of the no-eating notice pinned to the wall.
Five minutes, have a rest. Her comfortable
black face distracts me from the weeping windows.
How old are you? she asks out of the blue.

No way to wriggle out of revealing the truth.
A pause. *You don't look it – you're gorgeous.*
It's not true but I sit up straight and face tingling,
stuff the word in my pocket – it goes on singing!

PERSEPHONE IN FINSBURY PARK

One

She pressed her face against the carriage window as if
its cool glass and the October fields would soothe last night's
beetroot sting – not a bee sting though bees had been the trigger –
the sting her mother delivered. 'Minutes as a trainee,' she'd snorted,
'green as in raw, not fingers, yet you interrupted the top level meeting

that I'd slaved to set up and spouted like a fund raiser, almost wrecked
the afternoon.' At this point a rage, which Persi had got into the habit
of switching off when her mother turned spiky as the garden rake,
erupted like lava: 'I'm sick of being pecked by you, Cornelia Crow.
I spent most of the summer studying bee decline and safe pest control

so when we reached new initiatives I tried to present my findings
with Portia logic…' The slap on her cheek had stopped her mid-flow
but, furious, she shoved her mother hard. Then shocked –
they'd never quarrelled before – she'd rushed upstairs, locked herself
in her room and sobbed, overwhelmed by waves of conflicting feelings,

until the lucidity of a crescent moon emerging above the beech trees
in the front garden calmed her down and somehow filled her
with hope. She'd pointed out to herself that in spite of the ghastly row
she still adored Mum, believed in her work with the Agency, her mission
to fight hunger but she'd been wrong to dismiss her daughter's passion

for drama, take a dim view of studying it at college, wrong to persuade her
not to pursue the stage. Her own mistake was ignoring Foxtrot and Feather.
The twins, her best friends, had both urged her to unbuckle herself
from the life her mother had carved out and move into a flat with them.
'It's obvious you're not designed for glueing your arse to an office chair,'

Feather had insisted, 'you're star of a famous uni's dramatic society,
an actor, a mimic.' Determined now, Persi had spent the night packing
some essentials and psyching herself up to cut the tie with Mum, leave
the South Downs and campaigning for bees. When called this morning
she'd faked illness until Cornelia's car crunched on the drive, then grabbed

her case and rucksack and called a cab. For ten minutes on the train
she'd felt triumphant, then the row had butted in. Now a voice in her head
rapped: *smartass, you're a nothing, will never stand on your own feet.*
At Waterloo she defied it, dug out her phone. 'Buckingham Palace,' Foxtrot
mumbled sleepily. 'I've done it, I'm in London, can I come over?' Persi gulped.

Two

After hours serving in the *Knife and Fork Café* at the *Hound of Hell Studios* –
fun because of all the theatre talk – it was luxuriating to soak up to her neck
in the ancient bath surrounded by walls mapped with continents of stain.
Persi thought how her life had changed since the morning she stood
limp as a fallen leaf on the step of the old house where the twins

occupied the third floor plus an attic with a skylight which now belonged
to her. She loved kneeling on the elderly desk to gaze over muddled roofs,
some sprouting plants, even small trees. Her friends had pounced on her
as if she wasn't a waif, said they desperately needed someone to share
so she was the answer to a prayer. Her mother's machinations, their fight,

the Agency stiff with office-chat seemed years, not two weeks away
and the really fantastic thing was her audition tonight with Hamish –
thanks to Foxtrot who'd landed the job of assistant stage manager.
She'd gathered that Hamish was a person with ferocious energy: director,
playwright and adaptor who was determined to put *The Hound of Hell*

on London's theatrical map with a repertory of plays and a programme
of daytime performance classes. Yesterday like a deus ex machina
he'd appeared in the Café while she was chatting to Foxtrot in her break.
His hair was black as his jogging suit and his greenish eyes pinned her
to her stool when he said: 'Ah, the protégé, tell me about yourself.'

Feeling foolish she'd mumbled some words about *Uncle Vanya*
and taking it up to the Edinburgh Fringe. 'She's a brilliant mimic,'
Foxtrot put in. 'Good, give me a sample tomorrow. I need to get water
for Deadly.' He'd disappeared into the *Knife and Fork's* kitchen. 'It's rare
for Hamish to show such interest,' Foxtrot grinned, 'he was definitely taken.'

Persi was still unnerved by the encounter but Hamish was a magnet
pulling her towards the world of theatre. Entering it was another matter.
Commanding herself to keep her cool, she tried to stop her rising panic
by doing a once-over of a whippet-faced woman who'd snapped
at a Chinese girl in the Café for spilling a drop of coffee on her cake.

It only worked for a couple of minutes. Grimly, she forced herself
to focus on her chosen piece: Nora in *A Doll's House* – that wow
of a moment when she turned on Torvald to tell him in a grave voice
the reasons why she was leaving: *It's your fault I've made nothing of my life,*
I have been your doll wife… Useless, she wasn't Nora at all, simply Persi

mouthing in a flap, a dabbler just out of uni, head full of *English with Drama*.
It was time to forget the whole thing – she'd fail, be a titanic disaster.
Banging on the door made her jump out of her skin. 'For heaven's sake,
are you dead or slurping whisky? You've been in that bath for hours,'
Foxtrot yelled. 'I absolutely can't do it,' Persi blurted but she was ordered

to *screw her courage to the sticking point* and bullied out of the flat
onto a bus. It struck her the *Hound of Hel*l was more like a gothic castle
than an ex-church as they descended the spiral steps to the theatre
in the basement. 'I've no voice,' she croaked. 'Don't be daft, it's the fear,
sit down, breathe and sip this.' Foxtrot twisted the top off a bottle of water.

Minutes later she was alone on the stage in a spotlight. It helped a little
that all the house lights were turned off and the auditorium invisible.
From the darkness a disembodied voice told her crisply to begin.
She'd no idea what prompted her to lead in with Torvald, the pompous
small-minded husband, who'd dominated and humiliated her for years,

Torvald who'd always regarded her as a silly child. No longer a doll wife,
she said with authority: *It's your fault I've made nothing of my life.*
Relieved she'd taken control at last, clear-headed, she'd demolished
her husband sentence by sentence. When she turned to exit
from the doll's house for ever the house lights came on. Looking back,

she saw Hamish in the front row and a black retriever sitting upright
beside him. What he said surpassed any comment: 'I'm putting you
in the Christmas production and come as my guest to the gig tonight –
it's jazz.' Dizzy with hope she followed him and the dog (evidently Deadly)
to the bar where he bought drinks and the dog sat with his paws on her feet.

Three

Stuck on a malodorous tube train which had jerked to a dead stop
between Arsenal and Holloway Road, Persi felt a pang for the clean scent
of turf on Uphurst's chalky Downs, for harebells, tormentil and the sense
of space even though she loved being on the move in London, its faces
and voices speaking languages from all over the world. She tried to imbibe

the stillness of the aged but straight-backed lady in a purple sari sitting
opposite. It was impossible. Her mind was bubbling like a cauldron
with the *Studios*: the buzz of people coming in for performance classes,
her new self in the *Hound of Hell Company*, the demanding rehearsals
of Hamish's updated and satirical version of *A Christmas Carol*.

It was brilliant to have the challenge of playing all three Christmas Ghosts.
It struck her she looked like a ghost in the window opposite. Her long
chestnut brown hair was a mass of colourless fuzz, her face elongated
but empty, somehow sinister. 'You got the part,' Hamish had told her later,
'because your voice changes were brilliant and now you're picking up

on projecting differently.' Working with him was fuelling her life,
that and the invisible rope which seemed to link them, though she struggled
against its tug. Trying to disguise her interest, she'd asked Foxtrot
about his personal life. 'I think he's a loner. He never talks about himself,'
her friend said. It had struck Persi he might be guarding a secret.

Two nights ago after rehearsal he'd taken her for a drink and talked non-stop
about problems with the play until Deadly stood up and barked and he said,
'Ok Nightshade, we're going,' and then abruptly asked her to supper in his flat
on Sunday. She'd felt poppies blooming redly on her cheeks as she agreed,
hoping his main intention wasn't simply to get her to sleep with him.

Now, trapped in the underworld of tunnels beneath the maze of streets,
she prickled with anxiety in case he thought she'd stood him up.
The train sighed, dawdled on, and at last, breathless from hurrying,
she was groping her way down steps to his flat. When he opened
the door what she saw first were the book cases crammed to the ceiling

and a black cloak hanging on a peg which reminded her of a bird of prey.
But candles and cutlery were set out on a table and she could smell
meat baking in an oven. 'It should be ready in ten minutes – the meal,'
he announced stiffly. She took care to adopt a light tone: 'Is it chance
you both live and work in basements?' He smiled: 'I'll tell you something:

day and sunlight are hugely overrated. Places in the belly of the earth
feed into my brain – their suggestive shadows, corners, passages.
I need them when I'm immersed in directing or writing. Think about it,
germination doesn't happen in light. Night, that's when I love going out.
Often I walk Nightshade in the small hours. There's a vibration in the air

and sudden shivers of light in darkness trigger my imagination.'
His voice charged the flat with energy, even the black leather sofa
and its mound of garnet-red cushions seemed to throb as though
under the spell of an ancient religion. 'You could use those words
in a play,' she whispered. 'Maybe I will...' Hamish's eyes, glittering,

met hers for a moment. Then he glided away and returned bearing
platefuls of chicken quarters in a pepper-red sauce. Her 'delicious'
was brushed aside with: 'I cook on Sundays as a way of switching off.
Then he asked, 'When you chose *A Doll's House* for your audition
had you by any chance found out that I was planning to put it on

as the first play next year?' She shook her head. 'Well, I must have you
for Nora.' 'But you've got professionals...' 'You're still raw, it's true
but you instinctively inhabit characters and you're very teachable.'
He took her hand. She trembled with disappointment – she'd been a fool,
let herself fall into the stock situation. Face on fire, she countered:

'I suppose the *Studios* offer you quite a number of *teachable* girls.'
He snatched the empty plates. 'Rarely, and I'm in the habit of saying
exactly what I mean, I don't do seduction lines.' He marched out.
She heard him yell at the dog. This was followed by the sound of crockery
smashing and she remembered Foxtrot saying everyone was wary

of his mood swings. Appalled she'd insulted him, she peered into
the kitchen where he was picking up the pieces, whispered: 'I'm sorry.'
His face was expressionless and he didn't reply but she could tell his fury
had subsided. Tentatively she touched his arm. He looked at her then.
'Are you a Nora?' 'Sort of, my mum tried to manage me.' She trembled.

'I know all about hurt,' he sighed as he put a bowl of scraps on the floor
for Nightshade but didn't elaborate and she sensed some deep pain
he couldn't bear to name. Sitting on the sofa with dark chocolate cake
and coffee, they talked dramatists from Oscar Wilde to Alan Bennett,
relaxed. And now in this candlelit cave where she could almost imagine

bats folded in sleep, she longed to touch him, gave him a light kiss
as she stood up to leave. His lips found hers and she was aware
of a huge rush of feelings which had been missing in the feeble
on-off thing she'd had with Tom at college. He didn't try to detain her
but an inner voice warned her to be on guard or she'd be swallowed.

Four

Three weeks and not a word, her phone never switched on, texts
unanswered, three weeks since her good-natured but naïve daughter
had metamorphosed without warning and taken it upon herself
to stand up and start haranguing a crucial meeting. Back at home,
tensing like a lioness, she'd spat out: 'You're no better a mother

than Charles Dickens' Mrs. Jellaby,' and almost knocked her to the floor
before bolting to her room. Then next morning, after pretending illness,
she'd made a getaway as if escaping from a jailor. Cornelia threw off
her duvet patterned with faded grapes. Sleep was out of the question,
quite apart from the worry she missed Persi every minute of the day.

Suppose she'd had a breakdown or, cold and hungry, was bedding down
on a pavement and at this very moment letting herself be raped by a man
stinking of beer. Ghostlike, she wandered the house. It had helped a bit
that Jupe, who normally ignored voicemail, had registered her message
and phoned. Amazingly, he'd even driven his Merc down from London

and, instead of blowing his top, had cooked dinner and cajoled her into eating.
She had a blurred memory of him pouring port, kissing her neck and pulling her
into bed but he'd dashed off next morning, not bothered to ring since.
To calm herself she switched the TV on and her attention was caught
at once by two sets of twins being interviewed. Persi had mentioned friends

at college who were twins. She tried to remember their odd names
but the phone butted in. 'Well, have you traced her?' Jupe, obviously
in a thunderous mood. She didn't reply. 'It's your fault Persi fucked off,'
he snapped, 'you over-influenced her studies and I told you at the time
it was a mistake to push her into your choice of career. The world's needy

trouble her but she's not obsessed like you.' 'Part-time husband and father,
you barely know the girl but trust you to barge in and badmouth her mother.'
'I know her heart was set on the theatre, know she has genuine talent –
and for god's sake stop needling, I've always been straight with you
about my lifestyle and work taking me overseas. You're a gutsy woman,

you'd have packed me in twenty years ago if you were pissed off.
The truth is you're always over the moon to see me and wild for me
in bed.' His self-satisfaction was the final insult: 'I'm sacking you now!'
He laughed, 'No doubt you'll let me know when you change your mind.'
'Just bugger off!' She hurled the phone to the far end of the room,

then although she rarely drank, she gulped half a tumbler of gin.
Insufferable Jupe didn't matter but was it possible that Persi, who'd loved
growing crops in the garden as a child and always worried about the hungry,
hated her? In any case acting was such an insecure profession.
Huddled on the sofa, Cornelia suddenly felt dizzy. She closed her eyes

only to see her daughter slowly descending spiral after spiral of stairs
to a stage where she stood declaiming to tiers of crimson chairs.
Sitting on one, as if in judgement, was a black retriever. Waking
with a start, she tried to dismiss the dream. On the screen a peasant
was holding out a plant with long shrivelled leaves and talking sadly

about losing his cantaloupes. A sense of defeat overwhelmed her:
ever more people were starving, her work at the Agency was a drop
in the ocean and perhaps she really had driven away her daughter.
She shivered: before her seemed to stretch stooks of blackened wheat,
miles of melonless fields and Persi disappearing into the far distance.

Five

When the alarm broke into her sleep off Persi found she was bundled up
inside her duvet. Rain was tutting on the sullen skylight like a martinet
but she ignored it, glad she could linger in bed for a few minutes
as yesterday's discomforting rehearsal had kept her awake for hours.
In her seven weeks at the *Studios* she'd always left feeling upbeat,

her mind spinning with ideas about the play, Hamish's rigorous directing
and their growing relationship but yesterday Dan, the weedy guy
playing Bob Cratchit who'd been away ill for a week, had turned up
croaking about the bloody flu and not being ready yet to give up and die.
Hamish had been gentle for a while, then quite suddenly lost patience.

'Being the character's not enough, the audience have got to hear you
for fuck's sake.' Dan had projected his voice but in seconds was choking
so Foxtrot suggested a break. She was bawled out. Twenty minutes later
Hamish sent Dan home, then barked: 'For the fit it's tomorrow at midday,'
and swept out like a Roman Emperor. Persi had itched to challenge

his unnecessary harshness, didn't dare so she'd tried to creep away
but he'd propelled her into his den which was stuffed with props and scripts.
Half pleading, half aggressive he'd begged: 'Stay with me,' stroked her hair.
They'd made love several times, always in here on the musty chaise longue.
He'd sounded desperate for comfort but she couldn't help saying:

'What about Dan?' 'I know, I know. In the morning I'll go to his place
with fruit and make sure he nurses his throat.' Relieved he was contrite,
she'd watched him lock the door. The sex was exciting but too rushed,
as it had been every time but last night she'd felt strangely like a puppet
he was controlling. Sensing he wanted to take her back to his flat,

she'd hidden her need to escape with a feeble joke about getting some rest.
When she'd finally slept she'd had bad dreams. In the last he'd ordered
Nightshade to jump on her bed. The huge weight of him on her chest
had made her struggle for breath as wadding seeped from her ribs
– no wonder she'd woken in such a tangle and sweating with fear.

When she reached *The Knife and Fork* she had a strong black coffee
but it didn't lessen her exhaustion and, unusually, the morning dragged.
Before the rehearsal began mutterings went round that the Black Prince
was still in a foul mood. There was no sign of it at first, Hamish was low-key
until they were halfway through the second scene of *Christmas Now*

but then he cut in testily: 'Wrong track, Ghost, and I've told you before
your keynote is cynicism not distress so bloody well sharpen up.'
Taken aback, Persi said, 'But surely I should be jabbing at Scrooge
with both?' 'Just follow my directions if you plan to continue in this play.'
The words tore through her like bullets and yet she heard herself say:

'But you've presented the whole scene as an appeal for the hungry so…'
'A fledging in the theatre yet you're so bigheaded you have the nerve
to hammer the director. Get out!' The order was roared. Holding in sobs,
she ran off the stage, up the steep steps and out into the street, ran
she'd no idea where. Her career was finished, her life ruined forever.

Six

It was gratifying, as she packed a few things for her trip to London,
to run through how she'd turned things round after the abysmal night
of the phone row with Jupe. She'd been trying to clear her aching head
next morning with a mug of dandelion tea and paracetamol when it hit her
she couldn't face going in to work so she'd got on the phone to Josh,

thanking god he was a first-rate deputy. Afterwards she'd gone outside,
breathed in the frosted front lawn, picked some sprigs of winter jasmine,
wished she was digging up leeks. Soon chilled, she'd retreated indoors
and picked up a card which was lying underneath the doormat, gasped
when she saw it was from Persi. Shaking she read: *Mum, I had to leave*

before we grew to detest each other. The bees were great but my first love
is acting. Guess what, I'm working in a small theatre. There was an address
but no date – it might have been lying on the floor for days. Weeping,
she'd admitted to herself she'd been too keyed up to register that Persi
had been quite brilliant in offering the meeting ideas she'd ferreted out,

a born speaker in fact. No wonder she had upped and fled from home
after being berated. Inwardly she'd snapped: Cornelia, start thinking.
The truth was the Agency had so taken her over she'd abandoned
her own life, stopped doing any proper cooking, given up gardening –
ignored her need to feel earth between her fingers, grow beans, carrots.

As for her social life – it had been nil. She hadn't even met up with Diana
for months although they'd been like sisters since they were children.
She should have turned to her two weeks ago. Disaster faced her
if she didn't have a complete break. The next morning she'd told Josh
she was burnt out and it was decided she must take a sabbatical at once

so she'd ended the week driving away from the stuffy Guildford office
as if freed from a cage. On Saturday, piling brunch on a pottery plate
of Diana's, she'd remembered her friend was now helping a small charity
in Malawi find outlets for colourful goods made by villagers and thought:
That's what I want: real life, coaxing crops from over-dry African soil.

She'd dialled straightaway to be greeted with: 'Cornelia, lovely to hear your voice – you've not answered my messages for ages.' They'd met for supper that evening and it only took one question to send Diana into rhapsodies about the visit she was making to the Ceres Aid villages in January to meet with craft workers but she interrupted herself to say:

'Look, this is a sideline – the charity's main need is for expert direction so they have the latest knowledge to help them produce more crops. Wouldn't this suit you? Suppose you come on my trip to Malawi with a view to spending a longer time there?' It had all been settled and now, only four weeks later, she was taking off to London to go

to the private view of an exhibition of Diana's work in a classy gallery, meet the director of Ceres Aid for a discussion, and best of all to pay a surprise visit to Persi. All she'd done so far was text her tactfully: *I'm really thrilled you've found a theatre that's offered you a way into acting*. She was longing to tell her how her own life had changed.

Seven

When she could run no more Persi paused, then walked on through street after street, seeing nothing but Hamish, his eyes glinting like a tiger's, hearing nothing but *Get Out! Get Out!* resounding like organ chords until ever larger droves of laden shoppers forced her to slow her pace and she registered she was at a standstill outside a store in Oxford Street.

Its windows beckoned with twinkling-eyed bambis and gilt-wrapped gifts in mock snow but they reminded her she was workless – she couldn't stay at the *Knife and Fork*. Her future was dead, a dodo. She zig-zagged away from the slurred come-on of a man who grabbed her arm, into a maze of side roads, was dazed to find herself walking through a street market –

an oasis in the middle of London. Pineapples queened it over grapes, a vegetable stall was heaped with ferny-leaved carrots, swedes and leeks. Suddenly she saw Mum in a muddy tracksuit puffing as she dug up sleek white vegetables with earth-clogged leaves, Mum gathering corn cobs – a mirage but this was her true Mum, not office-Cornelia. Stifling tears,

she stumbled on until daylight sank and cold, dizzy, she began to search
for an Underground station. Back at the flat the gentler twin, Feather,
was lying on the sofa reading but she couldn't bear to spill her hopelessness
so, mumbling she needed to crash out for a while, she clambered upstairs,
flung herself onto her bed. She didn't think she'd ever sleep again

but, exhausted, she dropped off at once only to have a sinister dream.
In the basement flat, now a damp cave, Nightshade was barking
and Hamish, his face white as a sheet, was crouched on a rock ledge.
Shocked, she reached out to touch him but he melted into her mother
who was frantically shelling peas. The green bobbles were overflowing

from the bowl into a cauldron. 'They're drowning,' Persi yelled and woke up.
Oddly, there was a smell of vegetables cooking downstairs. Her watch
told her it was ten past eight but she shook it as if it was lying – both twins
were going out this evening. Uneasy, she crept down to the kitchen,
pushed the door gingerly. At first she wondered if she was hallucinating.

The table was a cornucopia of mangoes, cherries, olives, roses in a jug
and standing by it was her mother, not in a tailored suit but a jazzy
orange dress. On the stove the large pan was steaming. 'You're *really* here,'
she burst into tears. Cornelia hugged her. 'I wanted to surprise you,
one of your twins let me in and said you were asleep so I made a stew

after nipping out to a shop for vegetables where I had a chat about yams.'
As it was ladled out Persi realized she was shaky with hunger. She ate,
almost forgetting herself as her mother enthused about her plans, agreed
going to Malawi was a great idea. 'Persi, you're a charismatic speaker,
you could be useful to Ceres Aid.' Though this wasn't exactly an apology

it showed Mum now viewed her as an adult. 'I'll help, of course,' she said,
appalled by the irony. She'd achieved nothing, was now a minnow adrift
in a hostile sea. Trying to disguise her misery, she smiled weakly
but Mum didn't miss it. 'Whatever's the matter? You're terribly pale,
look as if you haven't slept for weeks with those rings under your eyes.'

She blurted it out in staccato sentences: how she'd infuriated the director
this morning, lost her part in the play and her job at the *Studios* café.
Cornelia frowned. 'Surely not, it sounds as if he momentarily lost his temper –
don't make mountains, phone him, it will work out. I need to go soon,
I'll call you.' She doubted Mum was right but hope rose like a faint moon.

Eight

After Cornelia left Persi found a card by the roses and on it scrawled:
Call me. Urgent. Hx. Trembling, she listened to six phone messages.
Most demanded why the hell she wasn't answering but in spite of the tone
it was obvious Hamish was worried, the last was lugubrious and ran on.
'I'm lying in my wretched bed. It's the witching hour, Deadly's snoring

but I won't get a second's sleep unless I know you're ok. We're rehearsing
tomorrow at twelve, can't take Sunday off, it's three weeks till we open.
Be there for god's sake and let me come for breakfast, I'll bring rolls
from a fabulous baker.' In tears she told herself she'd been a total fool,
he really cared about her. She texted him in block capitals, then climbed

onto her desk and gazed at the thousands of lights glimmering like stars,
a mysterious otherworld which came to life when darkness stubbed out day.
Soothed, she slipped into bed without undressing, slept dreamlessly
until persistent ringing on a bell startled her awake – Hamish. She tore
down the flights of stairs. 'So you've not disappeared into thin air, Persi,

I hope you've forgiven me now?' She hesitated, half-wanting to hug him
and the large bag of rolls but yesterday's steamrolling was still lodged
in her head, the snarling at Dan too. She couldn't wipe his behaviour away
as if it didn't matter. 'Have you forgotten you sacked me from the play?'
Tense, she led the way up to the kitchen, half expecting a surge of anger

but, almost as white-faced as he was in her dream, he sat down wearily.
'I'd no idea you'd take me literally, do an Ariel – and look, you did attack
my authority as the director in front of the cast.' That's it she thought,
he can't bear being challenged in public, sees it as a putdown. 'Maybe
it wasn't the best time but surely at some point it would have been ok

to discuss with you what I believe is at the heart of the ghost character
in your version? I mean, do you think a director ought to be a dictator?'
Instinctively she stepped back in case he exploded. Instead he groaned:
'You're right. I suppose the truth is when I feel my control's threatened
I totally lose it, then afterwards I hate myself. What can I do about it?'

Childlike, he turned to her, grasped her hand. She knelt down beside him:
'Talk to someone – me. That night I came to your flat you told me you know
about hurt. What is it?' He sank into such a deep silence she thought
he was out of reach but at last he mumbled, 'I will but there's no time now.'
She put the kettle on, believing she'd learn soon what it was he was hiding.

The last weeks of rehearsal were full on and Hamish often snapped
but Persi noted he didn't lose his temper. However, every time she tried
to get him to open up he fobbed her off with an excuse. The first night
was a triumph yet after calls for the director and thunderous applause,
just when she least expected it, he created an unnecessary crisis

by collaring Joe whose choreography of the lighting was a work of art.
'What the hell were you doing,' he raved, 'to let the stage black out
for thirty seconds?' 'I can't stop sudden reductions in the electricity flow,
I'm not God,' Joe retorted, 'and anyway the total dark mesmerized
the audience. You can bloody well find someone else to light your show!'

Sickened, Persi stood by, was relieved but embarrassed when Hamish
grovelled. As they were leaving the *Studios* he asked her in a voice taut
as a tea-strainer to come back to his flat. 'Whatever the hurt is, tonight
you must tell me.' 'It's not pretty.' The distress in his charismatic face
drew her to him more than ever. In the basement he poured brandies,

then catapulted into his story: 'My father was my hero until I was seven,
then he began having violent mood changes. He'd be joking one minute,
the next, face flame-red, he'd hit out with a book, binoculars, anything
he could lay hands on. One afternoon while Mum was out shopping
he went for me and my twin swinging his toolbox hammer and yelling:

Which one of you two has stolen all the money that was in my wallet?
I'm giving you thirty seconds to confess or I'll kill both you little buggers.
We stood paralysed as he counted down but our elder brother appeared
and saved us by grabbing the weapon. Two men came and took Dad away.
He was different when he came back – it must have been months later –

but he often sank into a blank silence. The family kept up a pretence
that things were ok but Dad's hammer always seemed poised above me,
I never felt safe.' Persi stroked his arm, 'You couldn't possibly after all…'
Impatiently he cut in: 'Don't you see, I'm afraid I'm like him so I've never
trusted myself to let anyone get close – I thought you were my chance,

that with you in my life I'd get a grip on my temper but I'm still fucking up.'
'You're not, you've survived brilliantly from terrible damage.' Though shocked
by his story, she felt in charge. 'Now you've told me about the trauma
and the fear you've carried you'll find more ways to manage your anger.'
The storm within him seemed to quieten. He hugged her: 'Don't leave me!'

Nine

'Oh Doll, I'm so squeezy-weazy happy!' Persi loved picking up
fragments of conversations and the frilly, high-pitched female voices
distracted her from the thoughts circling in her head like disturbed birds.
When the pair of high-heeled, mink-coated women were out of hearing
she giggled, then tottered a few steps on the tips of her trainers mimicking

their voices. Her amusement faded quickly. In one sense it was true
she was squeezy-weazy happy. Last night she and Hamish had lain side
by side in his bed holding hands and he'd said: 'I'd no idea it was possible
to be closer than sex – I feel as if I'm knitted to you'. 'Touching like this
is more than words, than anything,' she'd whispered. After a while

they'd both dropped off, slept deeply as children till Nightshade scratching
at the door wakened them in the morning. Reluctantly, Persi had dressed
and taken herself off to the *Knife and Fork* where everyone was buzzing
about the play. A group talking loudly over coffees after a dance class
had called her over to their table to tell her she'd been absolutely amazing

and Foxtrot had scurried in bubbling with the news that Demetrios Mellor
was going to feature *The Hound of Hell* in *The Stage* which was thrilling.
But she'd kept picturing the terrified children, the father mentally ill,
the raised hammer, and wondered if she had the confidence and skill to help
Hamish. When she stopped work she'd hopped on a bus to Regent's Park

hoping a walk would clear her head but the trees were half lost in mist
and she couldn't quell her anxiety: Hamish's parting: 'Never leave me,'
had verged on the aggressive and it made her feel trapped again.
In addition she suspected her beloved pushy mother, who was coming
to tonight's performance, had some kind of plan to spring on her.

Eight hours later she was wedged uncomfortably behind a table
eating roast duck with sage sauce in a Victorian pub minutes away
from the *Studios*. The *Evening Standard's* rave review of the show,
its verve and biting humour, the mention of her as *a versatile young actor*,
tonight's many curtain calls, Mum enthusing about her performance,

had all drained away like water from an unplugged sink. Hamish
was treating them both to supper to celebrate but it was purgatory.
Cornelia had picked up in two minutes that his interest in her daughter
was much more than professional. Suddenly, and in a voice stiffer
than glacé icing on a Christmas cake, she said: 'The theatre's seasons

are quite short and there are no shows in high summer so I hope
you'll keep your promise to Ceres Aid, Persi. You're super at conveying
ideas. If you give a few fundraising talks you'll receive a small fee
and be flown out to Malawi for a month…' Hamish sliced into the flow,
'But everything tells me, Persi, that your soul is wedded to the theatre.

I really want you to start running mime and mimicry classes in January,
then put on a similar series in the school holiday project I run for kids.'
He pressed her hand under the table: 'In any case, as I'm sure you know,
you're indispensable.' Cornelia glared: 'Does this man dictate what you do?'
'Bloody shut up, shut up, I'll decide my future!' Persi's heart thumped

like a guitar. Shocked, she saw the other diners had stopped eating
and were staring but she couldn't bear it – the two of them tugging
for her as if she was a commodity. Trembling, she watched Cornelia,
tight-lipped, stand up and go to the cloakroom. Hamish looked crestfallen.
'I thought you were mine, Persi, how do I keep you?' 'Don't try to clamp me

to your life. If I feel I'm a free agent, if I'm trusted I'll come back to you
even if I've travelled to the ends of the earth.' He went quiet but she sensed
he understood. 'Where are you thinking of sleeping tonight?' he murmured.
'With you in your bed.' She nudged him to warn that Mum was returning.
A corner of the tablecloth lifted and Nightshade sat up, as if approving.

'Are large dogs allowed in here?' a sour-faced woman demanded,
Gazing at the pom-pom waggling on her beret, Persi echoed her tone:
'Absolutely, cats and rabbits too.' The three of them watched her tutting
her way out, then started to laugh. It broke the tension and by the time
the chef's dessert appeared Persi had said she was up for taking

mime classes, would fit in some talks and a short visit Malawi. The dessert
was a fantasia of pomegranate halves, berries and pistachio icecream.
'It's hard to dig them out the seedy flesh,' Persi laughed as she tussled
with one of her halves. It flew off her plate. She stooped. 'Too late,'
Hamish grinned, 'Nightshade thinks any food on the floor belongs to him.'

THE END